VANCOUVER SCHOOL OF THEOLOGY

40p

Contents

AF732100

The Members of the Commission

The Reverend Canon R. C. D. Jasper, M.A., D.D., F.R.HIST.S., *Chairman*
The Bishop of Newcastle
The Right Reverend H. E. Ashdown, D.D.
The Provost of Derby
The Very Reverend R. A. Beddoes, M.A.
The Bishop of Derby
The Right Reverend C. W. J. Bowles, M.A.
The Reverend C. O. Buchanan, M.A.
The Reverend Canon G. J. Cuming, M.A., D.D.
Mr D. L. Frost, M.A., PH.D.
The Reverend D. C. Gray, T.D., A.K.C.
The Dean of Bristol
The Very Reverend D. E. W. Harrison, M.A., D.LITT., *Vice-Chairman*
Mr T. S. Horan
The Reverend J. L. Houlden, M.A.
Mrs J. M. Mayland, M.A., DIP.TH.
Mrs E. M. Montefiore, M.A.
The Reverend Canon P. C. Moore, M.A., D.PHIL.
The Reverend L. E. H. Stephens-Hodge, M.A.
The Reverend Canon C. V. Taylor, M.A.
The Reverend Canon E. C. Whitaker, M.A.
Miss M. D. Fraser, B.A., M.TH., *Secretary*

CORRESPONDING MEMBERS:
The Bishop of St Edmundsbury and Ipswich
The Right Reverend L. W. Brown, D.D.
Mr Alan Wicks, MUS.BAC., F.R.C.O.
The Reverend J. D. Wilkinson, M.A.

1. Introduction

During the past four years the Liturgical Commission has collected a great deal of comment and criticism on Series 2. Some has been obtained first-hand, for many members of the Commission have given generously of their time in speaking about the rite all over the country. We have also received hundreds of letters; and as a matter of policy we have tried to answer all the questions which have been put to us. Thirdly, we have studied in co-operation with the diocesan committees the answers to some two hundred thousand questionnaires which we sent out two years ago. All this evidence has been invaluable in producing Series 3; and at the same time we have considered carefully the points made by the Convocations and the House of Laity when Series 2 was first authorized for experimental use. As a result we believe that we have remedied the weaknesses in the rite which experience has brought to light.

Inevitably the question is bound to arise, 'What next? We have had Series 1, 2, and 3. How many more experimental services must we endure?' The answer will, I hope, be reassuring. It is our desire to regard Series 3 in general as definitive. After experiment small modifications and improvements may be found necessary; but we hope that we shall not be obliged to undertake yet another major piece of revision, and that we shall be able to incorporate nearly all of this new rite with other new services in a Prayer Book by about 1975-76.

One criticism levelled against Series 2 was the lack of accompanying explanatory material and music. This we have now tried to remedy in a number of ways.

1. This present commentary is much fuller than anything we produced with Series 2; and if the new rite is ultimately found acceptable, we should like to produce a major commentary, setting out in detail the theological and liturgical basis for what we have done.

2. A working party, appointed jointly by the Liturgical Commission and the Council for the Care of Churches with the approval of the Archbishops, is producing (*a*) a filmstrip and commentary, and (*b*) a small book on 'The Presentation of the Eucharist: Series 3'—simple and practical guides to help parishes with their use of the new rite.

3. Music will be available at the outset. One great advantage of the ICET Texts is the interavailability of music between the Churches; and already the Anglican, the Lutheran, and the Roman Catholic Churches in America have published settings which we can use with Series 3 in this country. In addition, settings are now being produced in England and these should be available by the time the service is authorized. Work is also being done on an 'Altar Book' with the necessary chants. Further information is included at the end of the commentary.

R. C. D. Jasper.

2. *The Guiding Principles of Series 2*

Holy Communion: Series 2 was produced by the Liturgical Commission as an experimental rite. Our terms of reference in respect of it encouraged us to be 'radical'. Furthermore, the whole constitutional position under the Prayer Book (Alternative and Other Services) Measure 1965 seemed to demand alternative services which would be relatively short-term experiments contributing to the fourteen-year trial period permitted by the Measure. The provisional nature of Series 2 was further emphasized by the speed with which it had to be completed. An unfinished draft text was included as an appendix in *Alternative Services: Second Series* in December 1965, simply to indicate the lines on which the Commission was working; but at the Liturgical Conference of the Church Assembly in February 1966 the Commission was urged to complete the text with all speed. They did this at one session in March 1966, fully aware that the result was far from perfect. At the request of the Liturgical Conference certain 1662 material (e.g. the Commandments, the Words of Administration, and the Blessing) was also incorporated into the text. It was recognized that these elements might help the transition into the use of experimental texts; but the Commission left open the question whether they should remain as permanent features in the Church of England's worship. Because they were regarded as optional, they were able to 'find their own level'.

The debates in the Convocations and the House of Laity between May 1966 and July 1967 (when the service was finally authorized for four years' experimental use) resulted in the introduction of other provisional elements into the text. The doctrinal controversies over the prayer for the departed and the oblation of the bread and cup were solved by stop-gap expedients. The compromise texts have proved more unitive in practice than many critics would have expected in 1967; but they were intended to allow sufficient time to examine the problems more thoroughly, without depriving the Church of the opportunity to experiment with a new structure of service.

It would appear that, because the Church of England has for three centuries had a single, uniform, authoritative Prayer Book, many worshippers have never grasped the experimental character of Series 2. They have never really *experimented* with the various options, and all too often their experience has been limited to only one form of the service. Furthermore, whereas they have been able to adapt themselves—perhaps with difficulty—to a particular set of changes involved in Series 2, they have not always been aware of the larger adjustment required to *living with change*. Now, as Series 2 approaches the end of its legal life (by a decision of the new General Synod it will expire in July 1972), one round of experiment closes and the next round starts by building on the lessons learned since 1965.

A Structured Rite An obvious feature of Series 2 was its structure. Clear headings marked off the 'Antecommunion' from the 'Communion'—the Bible service from the meal. In the Bible service the readings from Scripture and the sermon were the centre of the liturgy. The introduction was almost entirely optional and the Creed and the prayers were a response to the ministry of the word. In the service of the meal the sacramental actions were grouped into a unitary sequence. Thus the table was laid, the thanksgiving was said over the bread and the cup, the bread was broken, and then the elements were distributed. All these actions were marked out by the subordinate headings, so that the structure was visible at a glance. The penitential section was appropriately placed after the intercessions as an approach to the table, while the conclusion was simply a liturgical departure from the service. This basic structure of the service is an important aspect of the convergence of understanding about the Eucharist which is to be seen throughout Christendom; and in the light of the experience of Series 2, we have found no good reason to depart from it in Series 3.

A Rite with Options Series 2 stood in marked contrast with the 1662 rite in the number of options and alternatives it allowed; only a minimum was mandatory. The service could be as short as fifteen minutes, or as long as an hour and a half; and it has been the delight of some critics to mock at the astronomical number of variations of the service which could be devised. Nevertheless, experience has shown that these varying possibilities do not in fact disturb a basic structure which can still easily be followed; and a change of route need never involve a loss of way. Indeed, the existence of options has proved valuable for a number of reasons:

(i) It has enabled new features (such as the Old Testament lesson and the Peace) to be introduced smoothly, without any sense of compulsion.
(ii) It has enabled the cautious to begin by assimilating Series 2 as closely as possible to 1662, and thus to get used to it.
(iii) It has allowed for an acceptable shorter form for use on weekdays, as well as for the full form for use on Sundays.
(iv) It has recognized the local congregation as a mature and responsible body, capable of making its own decisions on matters of detail in the forms of worship which it uses.

The Commission therefore does not regret the range of options which were provided in Series 2. Nevertheless, the experience of the past four years and the evidence provided by the questionnaire have enabled us to identify places where options are not now needed, as well as to introduce new elements (particularly the seasonal material) for optional, experimental use during the coming period.

Eucharistic Theology The theological purpose of Series 2 was to provide a rite which would permit differing emphases of understanding of the sacrament without excluding any legitimate standpoint. The aim was devotional and liturgical, not didactic and confessional. A liturgy is not necessarily the best place for precise theological statement. In the event the changes made by the Convocations and the House of Laity may have fulfilled these aims better than the Commission's original text; and the Commission itself duly underwrote these changes. Admittedly Series 2 appeared to treat some issues more lightly than 1662, and particularly the nature of the atonement; nevertheless, it treated others in a far more satisfactory manner than 1662. Thus the references to baptism, to the unity of the Church as consolidated and expressed in Holy Communion, and to the 'mighty acts' of God in creation, in Christ, and in the giving of the Spirit, are sheer gain.

The Commission would not wish to stop there, however. The reshaping of the structure of the service in Series 2 was not just liturgical or psychological; it was also doctrinal. The sense of making a corporate thanksgiving over the elements has been a great improvement on the provisions in 1662. The whole action is now seen as that which sets apart—consecrates—the bread and the wine for their God-given use, in accordance with the commands of Jesus Christ. The great prayer of Thanksgiving both verbalizes our intention and actually makes the service the Lord's Supper. This overall structure has been the most notable feature of Series 2; and it is from this starting-point that the Commission has undertaken its work on Series 3.

3. *Language*

The Liturgical Commission shares the Church's love and respect for the language of the Book of Common Prayer, but realizes that there are pastoral situations for which it is unsuited. Some of its richness is now lost to all but the highly literate; its archaic diction can diminish attention and be a barrier to understanding; and its flavour may suggest to some people that the faith is a relic and not a vital tradition. Series 3 is now offered as a rite for those who desire to worship in a language closer to their own. This desire has made itself felt in all parts of the world, and the general trend in the new liturgies of all Churches is for modern language.

The change from *thou* to *you* when praying to God will be difficult for some people; but we must be careful to look at the problem in its true perspective. By a linguistic accident, the thou-form which was a highly intimate mode of address in Cranmer's day has become generally obsolete; but through its survival in prayers it has acquired a sacral tone which the Reformers did not intend. Many Christians now value it as indicating the transcendent nature of God. But the case for retaining thou-forms in modern liturgical texts must not be judged apart from those undoubted archaisms that such a retention would dictate—forms such as *thee, thine, thy, shalt, wilt, dost, didst, hast, art,* and all verb forms ending in *-est.* To avoid disturbing clashes between modern and archaic language, the whole syntax, rhetoric, vocabulary and tone of modern compositions would be forced back into older patterns. The result could only be a 'church diction' not fully in contact with the living language of either the sixteenth or the twentieth century.

We have not found it easy to meet the demand for a modern liturgical English, and we have eventually made new departures. It has proved impossible simply to 'translate' old material into twentieth-century English. We found ourselves left with bare bones, stripped of imagery, lightened of ideas, with the beauty and emotive power of admittedly outdated rhetorical structures and effects quite lost, and yet with nothing to put in their place. In consequence, we have done two things. In cases such as the Collect for Purity (4), or the Prayer of Humble Access (20), where there has been an overwhelming desire for much-loved material to remain, we have made only minimal updatings (on the analogy of R.S.V.), and we have tried to avoid literary vandalism. We accept that the flavour of such material will remain rather archaic; but we believe that this is not offensive in modern services provided the sense remains clear and the material is left harmonious with itself. It is, after all, axiomatic in architectural thinking that buildings of different periods will go together, provided each is in its own way excellent. We have also attempted to compose new material, which we may hope may have some beauty and point when laid beside the old, but which will achieve its effects in distinctively modern ways. We have tried, however, to avoid those concepts of 'modern language' which have produced such unsatisfying results in some modern Bible translations and in some liturgies. Good modern English is not necessarily *conversational* English; still less is it weak, unrhythmic cliché; and the vocabulary of worship should not be the language of daily chat. Vocabulary tests have shown that all classes of people understand a far wider range of words than they themselves use; and any good spoken or written discourse can be shown to have rather different characteristics when compared with those of ordinary talk. In our new material we have therefore tried to use language and techniques such as a modern poet might use; and we have not always avoided technical terms, since any specialized human activity has them and they are readily mastered in other spheres.

We have been conscious that in material which worshippers must use again and again there is a need for richness of association and beauty of sound. We have also been aware that religious ideas and emotions must often be expressed through metaphor and image; and for most of our ideas and images we have returned to Scripture and the sayings of our Lord. Through the centuries liturgical prayer has commonly been a tissue of scriptural allusion; and the rationale of our new material and its full meaning can be seen from the scriptural texts from which it is derived. A more detailed examination of the references behind these new compositions will be found elsewhere in the Commentary.

We have not been responsible for all the new material. Modern translations of texts we share with other English-speaking Christians have been produced by the International Consultation on English Texts, and these are referred to in the next section. Nor have we yet provided new collects. All Churches find it extremely difficult to write acceptable modern versions of prayers so dependent in their original form on a Latin or quasi-latinate syntax, which in modern English tends to sound unnatural. We are still wrestling with this problem. Again, there is at present no published liturgical Psalter entirely suitable for use with services in modern language; but we have such a Psalter in active preparation, and selections from it will be included in other Series 3 services as they appear. We hope that this will be an accurate modern translation of the Hebrew, yet designed specifically for liturgical use and indebted to much fine English translation of the past.

4. *The Common Texts* (Sections 3, 5, 13, 26, 29, 31)

There exists in the Roman Catholic Church a body known as the International Committee on English in the Liturgy, whose task it is 'to achieve an English version of liturgical texts acceptable to the interested countries . . . bearing in mind the ecumenical aspects'. In recent years the Advisory Committee of this body has been meeting with representatives of the Liturgical Commissions of the major Christian Churches throughout the English-speaking world. From their discussions, in which we ourselves have taken part, there came the decision to try and produce agreed versions of certain texts which could be used by all English-speaking Churches. A great deal of preliminary work was done by small groups in various parts of the world, and this was collected and revised by an international and ecumenical body known as ICET or the International Consultation on English Texts. This body has now published a set of agreed texts in a booklet entitled *Prayers we have in common* (Geoffrey Chapman). These are now presented to the Churches for experimental use over a period of years, after which they will be reviewed in the light of comments and criticisms received. Series 3 contains the following texts in this category—the Greeting (3), the Gloria (5), the Nicene Creed (13), part of the Sursum Corda (26), the Sanctus (29), and the Lord's Prayer (31). Already these texts have been adopted by a number of provinces in the Anglican Communion, the Lutheran Churches in America, several parts of the Roman Catholic Church, and a number of reformed Churches. Clearly the ICET proposals differ in some respects from what we proposed in our *Modern Liturgical Texts* in 1968 and from what we ourselves would have proposed now. Nevertheless, we believe it right, in the interests of Christian unity, to use these texts experimentally in Series 3; and we would hope to add our comments to those of other Churches when they come up for review in a few years' time. A full commentary on these texts will be found in *Prayers we have in common,* but the more important points are set out here.

The Gloria in Excelsis The *Gloria* is a series of acclamations, characteristic of the ancient Greek liturgies. Since it is not a dogmatic text but a hymn, a modern version is not bound to a strictly literal translation. The hymn consists of an opening antiphon based on Luke 2.14, followed by three acclamations, the first addressed to God the Father, and the second and third to God the Son. This translation preserves this structure, but transposes certain lines and phrases for purposes of clarity and omits others to avoid unnecessary redundancy.

Lines 1-2 The text is uncertain in Luke 2.14. The Eastern tradition refers —the 'favour' or 'good will' to God; but the Western tradition refers them to men—'God's peace among men of good will, or among men of his favour'. There is also the question as to whether 'men' refers to mankind generally, or to the people who are the recipients of God's special favour. The translation here agrees with RSV, NEB, and JB in regarding 'favour' as God's favour; but it leaves open, in the phrase 'to his people' whether 'people' means all men or those who are specifically his people of faith and hope.

Lines 3-6 The order of lines 3-4 and 5-6 in the original has been reversed, to make it clear at once that the stanza is addressed to God the Father. We now have two pairs of parallel lines, coming to a climax in the word 'glory'.

Lines 7-12 The transposition of 'only Son of the Father' and 'Lamb of God' in lines 7-8 gives each of these lines an acclamation that praises Christ in both his divine and human natures; and it also places 'Lamb of God' in immediate juxtaposition with what follows appropriately in lines 9-10.

Line 9 The Greek manuscripts vary in the use of 'sin' and 'sins'. The singular has been adopted here, in accordance with the text of John 1.29.

Lines 13-18 The repetition of 'alone' is emphatic, to show that the titles here given to Christ are those which also belong to the Father—'Holy One, Lord, and Most High'. Lines 16-18 are a concluding trinitarian doxology.

The Nicene Creed Line 1 The use of the plural 'we' follows the Greek text of the original conciliar form of credal statement. It is appropriate in a creed spoken by the whole congregation; and it is distinct from the use of the singular in the Apostles' Creed, which had its origin in a personal profession of faith.

Line 7 'Eternally begotten'. In spite of some dissatisfaction with this phrase, no better alternative has been suggested. There are certain philosophical objections to the recent proposal, 'before time began'; while the older phrase, 'before all worlds', was felt to be too obscure and archaic. The phrase represents one of the statements in the original Creed designed to refute the denial of the Son's eternity and the assertion of his posteriority to the Father. For those who find 'eternally' too suggestive of an 'ongoing process', J. N. D. Kelly in *Early Christian Doctrines* (2nd edn, p. 243) points out that St Athanasius argued that 'the Son must exist eternally alongside the Father. The explanation of this is that his generation is an eternal process.' See also his *Early Christian Creeds,* p. 238.

Line 11 The Greek term *homoousios* is difficult to translate, but 'Being' seems preferable to 'nature' or 'essence' or 'substance' in a statement which tries to express the unity of the Godhead. Many consultants agreed that 'Being' came nearest to the Greek philosophical term, even in its etymology. The argument of the sentence is that, because the Son is not made but begotten, he shares the same kind of being as the Father.

Line 22 'In fulfilment of the Scriptures'. The Greek phrase is again not easy to translate, but 'in fulfilment of' is closer to the sense than 'according to'. The latter might suggest that Scripture says one thing, while other authorities says something different.

The Lord's Prayer The Christian Church has always used the Matthaean rather than the Lucan text of the prayer in liturgy; and here an attempt is made to produce a translation of Matt. 6.9–13 in which the style and even the words of the familiar version are retained so far as this is consistent with the elimination of archaic expressions and with the demands of clear and accurate translation. Two lines in particular call for comment.

Line 2 'Holy be your Name'. This may be a petition or it may be a doxology. If it is a doxology, it refers to the preceding line rather than to the two which follow; it is then parallel to such Jewish acclamations as 'The Holy one, *blessed be he*'. If it is a petition, it should be linked with the following lines. Then it has a profound eschatological significance and it is a prayer that something be done, whether by God or by man. There are weighty reasons for thinking that what is sought is the action of God—'Father, show yourself to be the Holy One; bring in your kingdom; establish your will; on earth as in heaven.' Nevertheless, similar Jewish usage indicates that a strong case can also be made for regarding the petitions as referring to human action—that men may so act that God's Name may be sanctified, his kingdom established, and his will accomplished. No absolute decision on this line of the prayer can fairly be made. 'Your Name be hallowed' probably keeps most of the options open; but apparently 'hallowed' has passed out of use or become debased in parts of the English-speaking world. Accordingly, 'Holy be your Name' is proposed; although it is realized that it tends to swing the interpretative emphasis towards the doxological understanding.

Line 9 'Do not bring us to the test'. Two errors must be avoided. The first is the misconception that God can be the agent of temptation; the second is that the original Greek word means 'temptation' as it is meant today. Scholars agree that the reference here is primarily eschatological. It is probably a petition for deliverance from the final 'time of trial', which in biblical thought marks the Last Days and the full revelation of anti-Christ. The peril envisaged is that of apostasy—the renunciation of the Christian faith in the face of the suffering and persecution which is expected to herald the final triumph of God's kingdom. It was also a very real peril which faced the early Christian under persecution. Yet a reference to any occasion of testing, when issues of life and death are in the balance, is not excluded. Either way, it is certainly not subjective moral temptations that are basically envisaged. The proposed translation seems to be the most adequate available; it is also in full agreement with the scholarship responsible for NEB and JB.

5. *The Seasonal Material* (Sections 1, 28, 37, 45)

One of the criticisms levelled against Series 2 has been the lack of variation at the different seasons of the year; and in particular the paucity of 'proper prefaces' was deplored. We have therefore provided seasonal additions at four points—at the beginning of the rite, before the *Sanctus,* after communion, and at the blessing. Of these only the 'proper thanksgivings' before the *Sanctus* are mandatory. The seasons or occasions covered are: Advent, Christmas, Epiphany, Lent, Passiontide, Easter, Ascension, Whitsun, Trinity, Saints' Days, Harvest, Dedication, and Unity. Some of these are not represented at all four points; and the use of the material at one point does not entail the necessity of using the material at the other points at the same time.

The Introductory Sentences will eventually be available for use not only at the beginning of this service but also at the beginning of *Series 3: Morning and Evening Prayer.* Here, if there is an opening hymn, canticle, or psalm, the Sentence should precede it.

The material to be used before the *Sanctus* has been called Proper Thanksgivings instead of Proper Prefaces, for here the latter title is misleading. In 1662 this presented no problem, since the invariable preface was concerned with giving thanks to God briefly and in general terms, and the proper preface specified the particular works for which he was to be thanked. In Series 2 the situation was different. The invariable preface traversed the whole history of salvation and proper thanksgivings were inserted at relevant points. The result was awkward and confusing. Here it is now proposed that all the Proper Thanksgivings should be said at the end of the invariable preface, in which all the mighty acts of God have been rehearsed, before going on to the *Sanctus.*

The Communion Sentences, like those of 1549, are all taken from Scripture. They are to be used after everyone has communicated; and their function is to crystallize the central idea of the particular occasion immediately before a short period of silence for prayer or meditation. If a need is felt for further sentences—particularly during the season of Trinity—the minister may select suitable passages from the lessons appointed for the day.

The Blessings have been modelled on the medieval episcopal blessings contained in such collections as the *Benedictional of Leofric,* but the compositions are entirely new.

6. *The Word and the Prayers*

THE CALENDAR AND LESSONS (Sections 7-11)

The lectionary for Sundays and other principal days as it is set out in Table 1 was originally produced by the Joint Liturgical Group in their report *The Calendar and Lectionary*[1] in 1967. In 1969 we incorporated the same lectionary in our report, *The Calendar and Lessons for the Church's Year.* It has therefore an ecumenical background. It has already been authorized for use in the province of South Africa, it is in use in the Free Churches of this country, and the Church of Scotland proposes to include it in the new edition of the *Book of Common Order.*

The Calendar Until a new Calendar Measure has been approved, we must of course continue to use the existing calendrical arrangements, and this is what Table 1 sets out to do. This creates one difficulty. The Joint Liturgical Group originally worked on the eminently reasonable assumption that the preparation for celebrating the Incarnation at Christmas should begin with lessons about the Creation and the Fall, and then trace the history of God's purposes of redemption and revelation through the Old Testament. Since the four Sundays of Advent are plainly insufficient for this purpose, the lectionary begins nine Sundays before Christmas. The difficulty arises from the fact that the Prayer Book lectionary for the last five Sundays before Advent is not fully used every year, owing to Easter being moveable. In order to ensure the continuous reading of the new lectionary on the four Sundays in Advent and the five Sundays before Advent, we therefore propose that the readings for the last five Sundays after Trinity (Trinity

1 This lectionary has now been published, with the lessons printed out in full in the Jerusalem Bible version under the title *Readings at Holy Communion* (Darton, Longman and Todd, 1970).

23-27) should always be used, and that the Sundays which may or may not be observed according to the date of Easter should be Trinity 18 to 22. While these proposals involve this difficulty, they nevertheless have one advantage over the existing arrangement—it will never be necessary to turn back to the Sundays after Epiphany in any year to supply the deficiencies of Trinity.

The Lessons Both Series 1 and Series 2 made provision for reading three lessons at the Eucharist, including one from the Old Testament; but apparently only limited use has been made of the provision. This may have been due to a variety of causes—undue length, unhappy choice, and lack of availability. But we have thought it right to continue to provide three lessons, even though the reading of only two might well remain the norm in many parishes for some time to come. We also feel confident that once the Church has been given the opportunity of using the new lectionary people will soon come to apppreciate its merits.

The Notes of Series 3 make it clear that the Gospel is still mandatory throughout the year, and when only two lessons are read there is freedom of choice between the Old Testament lesson and the Epistle. Nevertheless, we believe that preference should be given to the Old Testament lesson during the last five Sundays in Trinity and the four Sundays in Advent, for during this period it is the Old Testament which provides the thrust of the whole lectionary.

We have also provided for the use of this lectionary not only at the Eucharist, but also at Morning and Evening Prayer. This is to meet the situation in many parishes where the Eucharist and Morning Prayer alternate as the principal Sunday service. A coherent pattern of lessons may now be followed week after week, irrespective of the service at which they are read.

In general two advantages may be claimed for the new lectionary over the old. First, the passages have been selected to secure a coherence between the lessons for each Sunday such as we do not find in the 1662 Prayer Book. Secondly, the two-yearly course secures both a welcome variety from year to year, and also a wider selection of passages from Scripture. It would also be true to say that the passages selected from the Epistles in the new lectionary are more intelligible and more edifying than those of 1662.

We now turn to consider briefly the contents of the lectionary. In the nine weeks before Christmas the theme is determined by the Old Testament, revealing the movement from the Creation and the Fall to the Incarnation. During the traditional Advent preparation nearer to Christmas the prophetic witness dominates. Over the centuries Advent has come to have a double reference—to the birth of Christ and to the Second Coming— and both these themes are provided for. On the last two Sundays before Christmas the lessons are concerned with the two people most concerned with the coming of Christ—John the Baptist and the Blessed Virgin. The reference to the Annunciation at this time is very appropriate, and there is no reason why this should conflict with the traditional observance of the feast on 25 March.

From Christmas until Whitsun the lessons are controlled by the sequence of events in the incarnate life of our Lord. A few significant points can be noted.

1. While the Epiphany is still observed on 6 January, the visit of the Wise Men also appears on the Sunday after Christmas. In this way the event will be given added weight, and will be more widely noted than the weekday observance secures.

2. The first Sunday after Epiphany is devoted to our Lord's Baptism, for this is now increasingly recognized as having an important place in the Epiphany tradition. The following Sundays after Epiphany then deal with various aspects of our Lord's ministry.

3. On the first Sunday in Lent chronology is ignored out of deference to tradition and the Gospel takes us back to the temptations of our Lord in the wilderness. This sets the theme of the conflict of the king and his kingdom against evil for the rest of Lent. It should again be noted that the observance of the Transfiguration on the fourth Sunday in Lent does not preclude its observance on 6 August; and clearly the right place for this reading in Lent is to foreshadow the Passion.

4. The Gospel themes for the first four Sundays after Easter diverge in the two years. The Gospels in year 1 are devoted to the resurrection appearances and in year 2 to a series of 'I am' passages from St John's Gospel, pointing to the eternal Christ and his abiding reality for the Christian and in the Church.

During the season of Trinity the lessons are designed to express the continuing life of the pilgrim Church in the experience of the living Spirit of Christ. While they leave abundant room for variety in exposition, there is a general direction of Christian life and experience running through them.

For those who wish to read a more detailed discussion of these proposals, this can be found in the Joint Liturgical Group's report *The Calendar and Lectionary,* published in 1967 (Oxford University Press).

The Psalms There are three points in the service at which psalms are likely to be used—at the beginning (2), and between the lessons (8, 10). Since it is very unlikely that psalms will be used at all three points in any one service, we have provided only two psalms with every set of lessons; and either of the psalms may be used at any of the three points. In some cases it will be found that one of them provides an apt comment on one of the lessons, or that it looks forward to the Gospel. But to find psalms which match the lessons exactly in every case is not possible. Some of the psalms have therefore been chosen because they match the mood or character of the season, or because they form suitable introductions to worship as an introit. In any case the psalms are for optional use throughout; and a canticle or a hymn may be found to be more appropriate between the Epistle and the Gospel.

Tables 2 and 3 These tables set out in convenient form the Holy Days and other occasions which are listed in the Book of Common Prayer and in Series 1.

Table 2 provides for the Red Letter Days in the Book of Common Prayer, and with the addition of St Mary Magdalen, the Transfiguration, and three Black Letter Days from Series 1. For the most part the Old Testament lessons in this table are those of Series 1, and the Epistles and Gospels those of the Prayer Book and Series 1. We have taken the opportunity to make some amendments, however; new Epistles have been provided in about a dozen cases and new Gospels in two.

Table 3 makes provision for the festivals of martyrs, doctors, and other saints, and for the miscellaneous occasions which are listed in Series 1. In addition we have made provision for weddings, and for times of trouble or disaster.

It should be clearly understood that the contents of all three Tables are optional alternatives to the material provided in the Book of Common Prayer and in Series 1.

THE PRAYERS (Section 15)

We have attempted to improve and enrich the Prayers in a number of ways. In the first place, we have allowed for the inclusion of both intercessions and thanksgivings. Secondly, we have inserted an additional section to cover what is best described as the local community, which includes not only those with whom we live or work, but also those who are connected with us in a special or personal way. We have also modified the final section so as not invariably to exclude the commemoration of other departed apart from the faithful departed, and we have followed the lines suggested by the Doctrine Commission in their report *Prayer and the Departed* (pp. 53-5). Finally, in response to a great weight of comment and criticism, we have inverted the order, so that the versicle and response come after instead of before the set sections.

We hope that these changes, together with an improved lay-out will make the Prayers more acceptable. It is now possible to use this form in a number of ways:

(i) The set pieces may be used as one continuous prayer without any pauses for special intercessions or thanksgivings, and without any use of the versicle and response.

(ii) The set pieces may be used with silences after each section, without any special intercessions and thanksgivings, but with the use of the versicle and response.

(iii) The second form may be used with special intercessions and thanksgivings in any or all of the sections.

We have therefore thought it unnecessary to provide any other alternative forms; and during the experimental period the forms in Appendix 2 of Series 2 are still available.

THE ACT OF PENITENCE (Sections 16-20)

The Commandments (16) It has been urged that in the Decalogue we have a hallowed statement of fundamental morals, the value of which lies both in its contents and in the rich treasury of associations which has gathered around it for those who have come under its influence. It is sometimes argued that the regular use of the Decalogue in Anglican worship in the past has been of significant value to the life of the nation; and that the present lowering of moral standards is in some measure due to its neglect. It has also been held that in the pattern of the Christian faith, Law precedes Gospel; and therefore in the liturgy, when we rehearse before God the pattern of his saving works, we should include that which prepared the way for Christ. For reasons such as these some people would argue that the Decalogue should be retained in the Eucharist as a mandatory element. On the other hand, account must be taken of those for whom its presence in the rite would create a serious difficulty. Some would argue that the constant repetition of the Decalogue has led to the common but mistaken assumption that it is a satisfactory summary of Christian ethics. It is, of course, no such thing. It is only a basis, and needs expounding in the light of Christ. Whether it is regarded as a means to prepare Christians for worship or to urge them to penitence, it falls short of the vision which should be put before them.

We have attempted to solve the problems created by these various views by presenting the Decalogue in a fresh position and in a rather different form.

Its new position before the confession is suitable; and it both avoids the duplication of penitential material and reduces the incoherent collection of items which has accumulated over the centuries at the beginning of the rite. The requirement that it should be mandatory at least on Ash Wednesday and the first five Sundays of Lent is designed to meet the plea that the Decalogue should not be totally ignored. The New Testament passages which are appended to each of the Commandments set out at least one facet of the Christian understanding of the original command, sometimes interpreting and sometimes amplifying it. Apart from the two terms of our Lord's summary which they include (and which is therefore not provided as a separate form), it is not claimed that the New Testament passages add up to a complete summary of Christian ethics. What is claimed for them is that they lead us beyond the limitations of the Old Testament law to the grace and truth which comes through Jesus Christ.

The Introduction to the Confession and the Words of Comfort (17) Experience has shown that the Series 2 introduction to confession, 'Seeing we have a great high priest', has been received with very mixed feelings. Many people miss the 1662 reference to the 'commandments of God' and to 'love and charity with your neighbours', and regard their absence as an impoverishment. We have therefore produced a new Introduction which not only includes these elements, but also includes the basic ideas of three of the four Comfortable Words—or Words of Comfort, as we now prefer to call them. The Words themselves present something of a problem. We recognize that a substantial number of people no longer wish to use them, and do not regard them as absolutely necessary to the rite. On the other hand, there are others who are still very much attached to them and would be distressed if they were to disappear altogether.

We have therefore included them as a option in Series 3, but instead of being used after the Confession and Absolution, we have used them as part of the introduction to confession. Their content would seem to make them admirably suited to this position, for they provide the encouragement and confidence to make the confession. Furthermore, they now appear as part of the essential structure of the penitential section and not as a mere appendage to it. If, in the interests of brevity—and particularly on weekdays—some reduction in length is required, we have made it no longer necessary to use all the Words on every occasion. But it does mean that the Words, either in full, or in part, or in summary form, are used at every celebration.

The Confession (18) Although the Confession of Series 2 has been appreciated for its relative brevity, it has been criticized mainly because it failed to include any clear statement of sorrow for sin. Some people have also suggested that it is excessively brief. We therefore decided to make a fresh start and write an entirely new confession.

The new Confession owes a great deal to the inspiration of Dame Julian of Norwich, who observed that 'the Holy Spirit leads [a man] on to confession, so that he deliberately reveals his sins in all their nakedness and reality and admits with great sorrow and shame that he has befouled the fair image of God' (*Confessions of Divine Love,* 39). The reference to the giver of light and grace in line 1 recalls God's activity in creation and incarnation, and introduces the emotional implications of sinning against the light; it also links the prayer's opening with its conclusion, where we ask to be led out of darkness, so that we may walk as children of light. Though this final petition relates chiefly to our conduct on earth, it can also express a Christian wish for eternal light and life. The closing lines are also meant to link the Exodus, where God led the children of Israel out of bondage, with Christ's redemptive activity on the Cross, by which he leads us out from slavery to the powers of darkness into his 'own marvellous light'. The categories of sin in lines 3 and 4 are traditional, but lines 5 and 6 (borrowed from the New Zealand rite) rehearse those means by which we come to sin. Lines 7 and 8 sum up the effects of sin, both in what it has done to God, and also in what it has done to ourselves. These lines further express contrition, but in a hopeful context; they remind us that a loving God has made us in his image, with a glorious human potential restored by baptism, even if again 'marred' by human failing. Lines 9 and 10 express contrition and repentance, while line 11 gives the ground of hope in Christ. Line 12, in a phrase from the Book of Common Prayer which is too much loved to be omitted, asks that the past may really be 'past', forgiven and forgotten; and it implies an intention, with God's help, to put all present failings into that 'past'.

The Prayer of Humble Access (20) It is clear that the Prayer of Humble Access is so well-loved that it must be retained. We have therefore included it with the minimum of change. On the other hand, we felt it worth while to attempt to produce an alternative, and this we have done.

The comment has been made that such a prayer is not really necessary at this point, when we have already made a confession of our sins and received absolution. Nevertheless, some people still feel the need to express unworthiness as they approach the sacrament. The new prayer is related to George Herbert's 'Love', and we are also led to see ourselves as those unworthy persons whom the Lord of the Feast in his love sent for and 'compelled to come in'. Lines 3 and 4 recall the words of Psalm 24, 'Who shall ascend the hill of the Lord, and who shall stand in his holy place? He who has clean hands and a pure heart'; together with the injunction of St James,

'Draw near to God and he will draw near to you. Cleanse your hands, you sinners, and purify your hearts, you men of double mind' (Jas. 4.8). Lines 5 and 6 refer to the Canaanite woman who presented herself to Christ. In lines 7 and 8 the prayer moves us to remember that from the beginning God has been 'the God of our salvation', sending manna to the rebellious Israelites in the wilderness, and sending the 'true bread of heaven' in Christ, who shared his bread with sinners. It is then that we feel able to ask to be cleansed and fed by the Body and Blood of Christ, so that we may be incorporated with him; and we look forward to the messianic banquet which Christ promised and which communion foreshadows.

7. *The Communion*

THE PEACE (Sections 21-22)

The Commission remains convinced that the best position for the Peace is at the 'hinge' of the rite—after the prayers and before the Communion. As the sign of reconciliation, it follows logically after the act of penitence, and its position is also suggested by Matt. 5.23. This is the point also at which it appears as early as the second century in the *Apology* of Justin Martyr —'At the conclusion of the prayers we greet one another with a kiss. Then, bread and a chalice containing wine mixed with water are presented to the one presiding over the brethren.' In some rites the Peace came before the Offertory, and in others after the Offertory. We have therefore thought it right to regard the Peace as the preliminary to the eucharistic action rather than as the conclusion of the act of penitence, as in Series 2.

We have also considered it to be sufficiently important and acceptable to be made mandatory instead of optional; although the rubric is so worded that nothing more than the words need be said. But even though no form of handclasp is used, we feel that the words should be said with conviction, and that the very least the congregation should do for this part of the rite is to stand. The president's words have also been amended, and we believe Rom. 14.19 to be preferable to Eph. 4.3 as the exhortation following the statement 'We are the Body of Christ . . .'

THE SACRAMENTAL ACTION (Sections 23-36)

There is common agreement that the sacramental action in the Eucharist is fourfold—the taking of bread and wine, the giving of thanks to God over them, the breaking of the bread, and the sharing of the bread and cup. This pattern reflects the Church's practice from the earliest days, and that in turn was based upon the accounts in the New Testament of our Lord's action at the Last Supper. From the doctrinal point of view not all four elements are of the same weight. The Thanksgiving and the sharing are the heart of the rite; and it is in the Thanksgiving that we state the meaning of the Eucharist as a whole. For this reason we give the sense and the form of this great prayer a section to itself.

Here we deal with the other three parts of the action. The first, the taking of the bread and wine, is formal, signalling the beginning of the eucharistic action. The third, the breaking of the bread, attracts devotional meaning (e.g. it reminds us of our unity in our Lord crucified for us); but in the shape of the rite itself it is simply the necessary preliminary to the sharing which follows. The fourth and final act consummates the rite which the Thanksgiving has invested with all the solemn meaning which it possesses in God's purpose.

This shape was already laid out in Series 2; but we have tried to make it still clearer. We have omitted all directions for 'manual acts' by the president to accompany the narrative of the Last Supper. This narrative is one section within the Thanksgiving, and its function is to describe and give warrant for the action which the rite *as a whole* performs. To suggest a 'taking' half-way through the Thanksgiving is to frustrate the fourfold sequence which we follow, as well as to invest the reading of the narrative with a purpose and a meaning which we believe to be foreign to its proper use. We have therefore provided a heading and rubric for a 'taking' before the Thanksgiving begins; and we have distinguished this from the preparing of the table. At this point of 'taking' we suggest that the president should hold the vessels containing the elements above the table to mark the beginning of the sacramental action proper.

At the breaking of the bread we have now provided a shorter and more euphonious version of St Paul's words and made them mandatory. Again, we wish to make the pattern of the rite unmistakable; and the words indicate the central idea of the breaking, that it looks forward to the sharing in communion.

The sharing of the sacrament follows the reciting of the Lord's Prayer, as in Series 2. The invitation to communion, which has been widely used, is now mandatory. In its revised form it fully retains the traditional themes of the words of administration from the 1662 Prayer Book, and thus assists the doctrinal understanding of the sharing. The president and the other ministers should not receive before the reading of the invitation, for to do so robs their own receiving of this doctrinal backcloth and divides their communion from the people's. Nevertheless, there is no reason why the invitation should not be the cue for the people to move in order to receive communion. The rubric (32) has also been drafted to allow the sacrament to be administered to the people first, with the ministers waiting until last, if so desired.

For the words of administration we provide only one form—two short prayers, specifically addressed to each communicant. Seen against the backcloth of the invitation, we hope that these will be found acceptable; and the Amen is a much more natural response to prayer than to the very brief words provided in Series 2.

The traditional anthems, *Benedictus* and *Agnus Dei,* have been deliberately placed after the Communion in the hope that the pattern of the eucharistic action may stand out more clearly; but we recognize that they may be sung at various points in the service, as local conditions dictate.

THE THANKSGIVING (Sections 26-29)

Within the fourfold action just outlined the Thanksgiving holds a special place. Here we voice and define the meaning of the whole action. The other parts of the sequence take place with a minimum of verbal accompaniment: this prayer provides the characteristic *words* of the rite. Other ingredients in the service—Bible readings, intercessions, the Lord's Prayer—are found in acts of worship of many kinds. This prayer belongs to the Eucharist alone.

The Historical Background The deepest roots of this prayer lie in the blessing said by the chief person present at the beginning of a Jewish meal. The purpose of the blessing, or grace, was by an act of praise said over the food and drink to thank God for them. Sometimes the thanksgiving for those specific gifts was set in a longer prayer, in which God was praised for his many acts for his people—in creation and in the long course of their history.

Whether the Last Supper was strictly a Passover meal or not, its solemn character sets it clearly in continuity with such Jewish ritual. It is the praise of God which Jesus must have spoken over the bread and the cup at this meal; and we now follow his action. Yet we now do so standing at a distance of nineteen centuries, and receiving from our Christian past a strong tradition of how believers should best follow their Lord's example. Thus from earliest times Christians have brought together the thanksgivings which Christ himself offered over the two elements separately. We have accustomed ourselves to the responsive opening to the prayer, 'Lift up your hearts', etc., which we can trace back for seventeen centuries. Again, we invariably recite within this prayer the account of how our Lord instituted the Supper. We cannot and should not attempt to write the prayer without receiving these traditions of worship. When we write a new prayer today, we do so with clearly defined principles to guide us.

This does not mean that everything we receive from the second, the eleventh, or the sixteenth centuries is by its very venerability above criticism and reform. For instance, we now see the whole prayer as the second action of the fourfold sequence which we follow. It is the whole prayer which sets apart the bread and wine for their unique, sacramental use. If 'consecration' is the appropriate term for this setting apart—and it is a term which is not without its difficulties—then it is the offering of the whole thanksgiving over the elements within the context of the other actions of the fourfold sequence which 'consecrates'. If the thirteenth or the seventeenth centuries saw fit to have 'moments' of consecration at the recitation of the dominical words within the narrative of institution, we cannot now be bound by these precedents. History suggests that emphasis upon such 'moments' not only gives the rite a false climax at this point, but also distracts from the understanding of the prayer as being above all a *thanksgiving*; and if we lose that understanding we are failing in part to carry out our Lord's command to the best of our ability.

Series 2 and the Need for Further Revision The principles just referred to governed the writing of the Thanksgiving in Series 2. The elements of praise rang through its preface (the *Praefatio,* the telling out of the mighty acts of God). Jesus Christ stood at the heart of this praise as the agent of creation and the mediator of redemption. The praise reached its climax in the singing of the *Sanctus,* and this led into the words describing and authorizing the sacramental act itself. A petition for 'consecration' introduced the institution narrative; and the dominical command, 'Do this in remembrance of me', led equally naturally into an *anamnesis* paragraph in which the Church expressed its dutiful response. The general command 'Do this' was obeyed in the particular time and place with 'this bread and this cup'. In accordance with a strong Christian tradition the prayer then added a petition for fruitful reception and rounded off its theme of praise with a full doxology and the people's Amen.

Put this way, all seems well and sounds well. Nevertheless, the Commission came to the task of revision well aware that improvements were both desirable and possible. These have resulted partly from the improvised nature of the Series 2 *anamnesis* as it emerged from the Liturgical Conference in April 1967 and was agreed by the Convocations and the House of Laity. Other changes derive from clearly expressed desires for a fuller statement of the doctrine of the atonement, and also that in a prayer of this length, more congregational participation was needed. Other changes again have been due to the fact that the membership of the Commission has changed considerably since the creation of Series 2. Experts outside the Commission have also been consulted, including those engaged in studying various aspects of eucharistic theology in the Doctrine Commission. Like the writer of the Preface to the 1662 Prayer Book, we are tempted to assert that inspection will make the reasons for almost all our changes self-evident.

The Question of Alternative Thanksgivings The desire has been expressed in some quarters that the Commission should produce not one eucharistic prayer but several, or at least alternatives. In principle there is no reason why this should not be done, and the possibility of it remains. Different prayers may well cater for different occasions, which are not necessarily seasonal; or for different situations or congregations of different sizes; and the availability of a shorter thanksgiving might well be appreciated by some. The Commission is opposed, however, to any proposal to provide alternatives which are avowedly partisan. We noted the concern of the House of Laity to find a unitive rite in 1967, and we still believe this to be right. Whatever may appear in the way of alternatives in the future must be acceptable to the Church as a whole, and not simply to sections of the Church. The further period of experiment may demonstrate more clearly the need for additional eucharistic prayers; and the Commission is already considering possible ways of helping to meet that need.

The Structure of the Thanksgiving The prayer opens with the traditional dialogue of the *Sursum Corda.* Here we have written a new, rather free, but we think justifiable paraphrase of the initial salutation—*Dominus vobiscum: et cum spiritu tuo.*[1] This has the virtue of bringing out more forcibly the dynamic activity of the Spirit of God by which we offer our worship. For the early Christians prayer was a work of the Spirit (e.g. Rom. 8.26). To offer prayer acceptable to God, the assistance of the Spirit was necessary—it was a combined action of the divine and human spirit; and the literature of the early Church provides numerous references to this. We therefore believe it right to have the reference to the Spirit at the very outset; and, coupled with 'Lift up your hearts', the salutation in this form helps us to see the Eucharist as both a meeting with the Lord here on earth, and also an ascending into the heavenlies to meet him there. Series 2 has been criticized for the weakness of its reference to the work of the Spirit in the eucharistic prayer. We believe that these new opening words help to meet that criticism.

The rest of the first section contains a few changes in language from Series 2 but is otherwise not notably altered. The seasonal material in the

[1] We have discussed this in an earlier document (*Modern Liturgical Texts,* pp. 31-2); and it is clear that there is no general agreement on the precise meaning of these words.

'Proper Thanksgivings' covers a wider range of occasions than before; and we have now arranged that all these should come at the same place—at the end of the invariable Preface, when all the mighty acts of God have been rehearsed. The pattern is therefore much simpler and less confusing than Series 2.

The *Sanctus* is the version produced by ICET. The Commission is well aware that many people desire to sing *Benedictus qui venit* immediately after the *Sanctus*; but there are equally many who would find this unwelcome. Rather, therefore, than insert an optional item at this point in the prayer, which might cause muddle and provoke difference of opinion, we have decided to place it after the three actions of 'thanking, breaking, and giving', leaving freedom as to where it shall be used, if it is used at all. The prayer therefore proceeds as a single whole, and the *Sanctus* does not imply a break in sequence of thought. The link between it and the narrative of institution is provided by a paragraph corresponding to 'Hear us, O Father' in Series 2 and containing three main strands of thought, which we believe makes this section much clearer and more logical. The first phrase looks back to the previous praises of God; the second invokes our Lord's example and precept as our warrant for holding the service; and the third, 'grant that these gifts', expresses our dependence upon God who makes this solemn meal of bread and wine his sacrament of the body and blood of Christ. The narrative of institution now follows as before; and here we have ventured to translate perfect passive participles as present active indicative verbs—'I give' and 'I shed'—in the interests of clarity and simplicity. By saying as in Series 2 that our Lord gave thanks 'to you', we remind worshippers that this narrative falls within a prayer to God.

The desire for congregational acclamations at this point has been met by three brief statements which focus attention both on our Lord's death and resurrection, and on our salvation which arises from them and is not yet fully realized. These lead to the *anamnesis,* which is to respond fully to the Lord's command. Here the Series 2 phrase, 'We make the memorial', provided a temporary solution; but many people feel it is infelicitous, and it fails to echo our Lord's injunction as our new phrase does. By beginning the *anamnesis,* 'We do this in remembrance', the Commission has adequately incorporated the memorial theme and taken up the wording of the Lord's command. This left us free to employ a new verb in the next sentence—'we celebrate'—which we consider singularly appropriate especially in view of its popular background. The doctrine of the atonement is duly strengthened, and the new wording recalls St Paul's explanation of the Eucharist that in performing it we proclaim Christ's death until he comes. A shorter sentence structure means that another verb 'proclaim' is used in relation to the resurrection and ascension. Finally, the eschatological element is highlighted more fully by the phrase, 'the fullness of his coming in glory'. Here the verb 'look for' echoes the usage in the same context in the ICET version of the Creed.

After the *anamnesis* we offer 'this our sacrifice of thanks and praise'. This again reflects the character of the prayer as a thanksgiving and at the same time echoes traditional associations of the phrase with eucharistic worship. The petition for fruitful reception then introduces two further themes: the activity of the Spirit in communicating God's grace to us, and our unity in the body of Christ, re-established by our communion together. We regard the inclusion of these themes as an enrichment of what was provided in Series 2.

The prayer concludes with a solemn doxology and a congregational acclamation, which sets out the traditional pattern of Christian prayer and of this act of worship in particular. It is offered to the Father in Christ by the whole company of earth and heaven, inspired by the power of the Holy Spirit. God's glory is the overriding object of it all. The phrase, 'with all who stand before you in earth and heaven', calls for brief comment. 'To stand before God to worship or minister' is a phrase found in very early liturgical texts, for example, *The Apostolic Tradition of Hippolytus*; and it is clearly rooted in Scripture, where it indicated a worship not only of earth but also of heaven (Deut. 10.8; 18.5; 18.7; Dan. 7.10).

FURTHER CONSECRATION (Section 35)

Series 2 made no provision for the further consecration of one or other of the elements, if the supply proved to be insufficient. In the 1662 Prayer Book the relevant part of the narrative of institution had to be repeated, together with the manual acts. But such a practice is contrary to our understanding of the Thanksgiving as a whole, and perpetuates the idea of a 'moment' of consecration effected by a specific formula. The Commission cannot recommend a continuation of this practice. It is, however, clearly undesirable to repeat the entire Thanksgiving after taking more of the required element; this would not only be cumbersome, but in liturgical terms would constitute a separate sacramental action. This matter was also discussed at the liturgical debates of the Lambeth Conference of 1968, and here there was general agreement on the points to which we have just referred. We have therefore examined the whole question afresh, and in the course of our work we have also referred the matter to the Doctrine Commission. As a result we suggest the basic principle of bringing additional bread or wine into the sacramental action by associating them with the already consecrated elements, before the supply of the latter has been completely exhausted. For this there is good historical precedent.

The question then remained whether this should be done in silence, or with a brief form of words. In favour of silence, it may be said that it causes the least possible disruption to the continuity of the service; while in favour of the form of words, it may be said that it clarifies and defines what is happening and has a certain didactic usefulness. Neither we nor the Doctrine Commission could find any theological objection to either method; but we were unable to agree which should be adopted if only one method were to be provided. We have therefore provided a rubric which permits both methods; but we would not necessarily wish to resist the reduction of these two ways to one should the Synod wish to do this.

THE CONSUMPTION OF THE REMAINS (Section 36)

As in Series 2, provision is made for the consumption of what is left of the consecrated elements either immediately after communion or at the end of the service. This rubric leaves entirely open the questions involved in the administration of the sacrament to the sick and in reservation. These matters are being considered separately and we hope to report on them in due course.

8. *After Communion* (Sections 37-44)

In the final section of the rite we have been encouraged to produce a new post-communion prayer, to be said by one of the ministers alone. It begins by praising God because, when we 'were still far off', God came to meet us in the person of Christ and through him reconciled us to himself or 'brought us home'. In Christ the divine nature 'meets' human nature, both in the incarnation and in holy communion. In lines 1-3 the language is intended to recall Christ's expression of the nature of the divine love in his parable of the Prodigal Son. Lines 4 and 5 summarize the whole process and results of Christ's redemptive activity. In lines 6-8 we pray that, having shared in the sacrament of his Body and Blood, and as members of his mystical body the Church, we may live his risen life, and be his active workers in the world. Finally, in lines 9-12, in an image by which the writer of the Epistle to the Hebrews captured the paradox of free will, we pray that we may remain 'anchored' in the living hope of Christ, so that we ourselves may be truly free—willing slaves of Christ. Finally, in consequence of our freedom, we pray that the whole world may genuinely live, by praising God through Christ.

While this prayer is optional, the final prayer which has been slightly amended to include the element of thanksgiving is now mandatory, and is to be said by everyone. Unlike Series 2, in which the two prayers were regarded as alternatives, here one or both may be said.

Finally, the Blessing and the Dismissal have been transposed; and again, instead of being regarded as alternatives, the Blessing is optional and the Dismissal in a revised form is mandatory.

9. *The Use of Series 3 with Other Services*

The growth of the parish communion during the past forty years has meant an increasing appreciation of the public and social character of this sacrament. Indeed, because it is now recognized as a rite in which all those who are present share, we have deliberately used the term 'president' rather than 'priest' or 'celebrant'. He presides over the eucharistic assembly; and this assembly has been seen as the most common and accessible manifestation of the Church. So it has become increasingly common to include within its framework other actions of the people of God. The general principle to be applied to all these additions to the eucharistic rite is that the form of the Service of the Word should be left undisturbed. This does not mean that the lessons may not be those specially provided; but it does mean that other actions should not take place until after the Word has been proclaimed.

With Baptism, therefore, the rite would follow the sermon (12); and the Eucharist would be resumed at either the act of penitence (17) or at the Peace (21-2). The same procedure would also follow with the rites of Confirmation, Matrimony, and Burial.

It is also possible to relate the daily office more closely with the Eucharist. *Morning and Evening Prayer, Series 2 Revised* permits the psalms and lessons of the office to be regarded as the Service of the Word of the Eucharist. Furthermore, the lectionary appended to Series 3 may also be used at either Mattins and Evensong, or Eucharist. It therefore means that we have provided two shapes for the Service of the Word, with common psalmody and lessons and, if necessary, canticles. The main difference between the two shapes is that in the eucharistic shape the penitential section follows the lessons and prayers, while in the office shape it precedes them. In this way we hope that it will meet a need which has been expressed by many people.

10. Typography

An important aspect of liturgical revision which is sometimes overlooked is typography. Rites have to be presented in a printed form which reveals the intentions of the authors and enables congregations to understand them and to follow them easily. Series 2 went some way to meet these needs. It was a modest piece of typographical experiment; but we recognize that it did not go far enough, and in one or two places at least the text was not easy to follow. We therefore considered it important to seek expert advice on this matter in our work on Series 3 and to regard typography as an important element in the presentation of the rite.

Clear distinction has to be made between what is said by the ministers and what is said by the people, and between what is optional and what is mandatory; and guidance has also to be given at certain points on movement. To meet these requirements some interesting experiments have been made. At least one type-face not normally associated with liturgical work has been used, and there has been an unusual type-mix of Univers Light and Times Bold. At the same time the sense of the text has been allowed to override the traditions of the printer in filling every page from top to bottom. In this way arbitrary lay-outs have not been allowed to destroy the continuity or sense of the text. Furthermore, material which is optional or which is not used at every service has been arranged so as not to disrupt the normal flow of the rite.

The preparation of liturgical texts is a subject which has fascinated designers and printers since the invention of moveable type in 1450. This modest piece of work in connection with Series 3 will, we hope, break some new ground in helping to make it comprehensible and in giving it dignity.

11. Music for Series 3

At the time of going to press the following information about music is available.

1. Prepared by the Inter-Lutheran Commission on Worship in America: *Contemporary Worship 2. Services: the Holy Communion.* This contains four settings of the ICET texts, and is published by: Augsburg

Publishing House, Minneapolis, Minnesota; and Concordia Publishing House, St Louis, Missouri.

2. Prepared by the Protestant Episcopal Church of the U.S.A.: *Songs for Liturgy and More Hymns and Spiritual Songs*. This contains settings of the ICET texts, psalms, canticles, and hymns, and is published by Walton Music Corporation, 17 West 60th Street, New York, N.Y. 10023.
3. The Roman Catholic Church in America has produced four settings which include the ICET texts, and these are published by: The World Library of Sacred Music, 2145 Central Parkway, Cincinnati, Ohio 45214.
4. The Oxford University Press is publishing a Series 3 setting by John Rutter.
5. The Royal School of Church Music proposes to publish music for Series 3 and will publish details in the autumn..

12. Scriptural References

In order to save confusion and undue complications in the text, we have thought it best to include all the references to Scripture in a single section of the Commentary.

Seasonal Sentences (Section 1)
Advent: Isa. 40.5; Christmas: Luke 2.10, 11; Epiphany: Titus 2.11; Lent: Dan. 9.9; Passiontide: 1 Pet. 2.24; Easter: Luke 24.34; Ascension: Ps. 68.18, Eph. 4.10; Whitsun: Rom. 5.5; Trinity Sunday: Rev. 4.8; Saints' Days: Heb. 12.1; Harvest: Ps. 24.1; Dedication: Gen. 28, 16, 17; Unity: Ps. 133.1.

The Penitential Devotion (Section 16)
The Decalogue: Exod. 20.2–17.
Opening: John 14.15 and Luke 11.28.
Commandments 1, 2, 3: Mark 12.30; John 4.24; Heb. 12.28.
Commandments 4, 5: 1 Cor. 15.20 and Col. 3.2; 1 Pet. 2.16, 17.
Commandments 6, 7: Matt. 5. 22 and Rom. 12.21; 1 Cor. 6.19.
Commandments 8, 9, 10: Eph. 4.28; Eph. 4.25; Acts 20.35.
Ending: Mark 12.31 and Rom. 13.10.

The Summary and the Words of Comfort (Section 17)
The Summary: John 3.16; 1 Tim. 1.15; 1 John 2.1.
The Words of Comfort: Matt. 11.28; John 3.16; 1 Tim. 1.15; 1 John 2.1.

The Confession (Section 18)
Line 1: John 1.9; Rev. 22.5; Jas. 1.17.
Line 6: Isa: 53.5.
Line 7: Gen. 1.26–7; 5.1; 9.6; 1 Cor. 11.7; Rom. 3.23; 8.29–30.
Line 13: Col. 1.13; 1 Pet. 2.9.
Line 14: John 1.4; 12.35–6; 1 Thess. 5.5; 1 John 1.6–10.

The Prayer of Humble Access (Alternative form, Section 20)
Line 2: Matt. 22.1–10; Luke 14.15–23.
Lines 3-4: Ps. 24.3–4; Jas. 4.8.
Line 6: Matt. 15.27; Mark 7.28.
Line 7: Ps. 65.5.
Line 8: Exod. 16.4; Ps. 105.40; Luke 5.29–30; 7.34; 14.23; 15.2; John 6.31–57.
Lines 12-13: Luke 12.37; 13.29; 22.28–30.

The Peace (Section 21)
1 Cor. 12.27; 12.13; Rom. 14.19.

The Thanksgiving (Sections 26, 27, 29)
Col. 3.1–4; 1 Cor. 11.23–5; 1 Thess. 5.18; Eph. 5.20; John 17.11; Ps. 123.1; John 1.1; Heb. 4.12; Heb. 1.2; Gen. 1.27; John 1.10; Rom. 6.17–18, 22–3; Gal. 4.4; 1 Pet. 3.18; Rom. 4.25; 1 Pet. 2.9; Acts 2.33; John 6.63; 2 Cor. 3.6; 1 Cor. 12.13; Eph. 2.22; Isa. 6.3; Rev. 4.8; 19.1–6; Matt. 21.9; 1 Cor. 11.23–5; Mark 14.22–3; Matt. 26.26–8; Luke 22.19; 1 Cor. 15.3, 20, 22; 1 Cor. 11.24–5; Heb. 7.26–8; 9.6–14; 10.11–12; 1 Pet. 3.18; Acts 2.31–3; 1 Cor. 11.26; Titus 2.13; Heb. 9.28; Lev. 7.12; Heb. 13.15–16; Acts 2.42–7; 1 Cor. 10.17; Rom. 16.27; Ps. 135.1–4; Deut. 10.8; 18.5, 7; Dan. 7.10; Heb. 12.22–4; Rev. 7.9–12.

Proper Thanksgivings (Section 28)
Advent: Ps. 32.7 and Rev. 21.5 and Ps. 98.9; Christmas: Luke 1.35 and Heb. 2.16 and 2 Cor. 5.21 and 1 John 1.7; Epiphany: Heb. 1.3 and 1 Pet. 2.9; Lent: Wisd. 1.5 and 2 Pet. 2.9; Passiontide: Phil. 2.8 and 1 Pet. 2.24; Easter: 1 Cor. 15.55–7; Ascension: Acts 1.2–3 and Rev. 11.17; Whitsun: John 16.13 and Mark 13.10 and 1 Pet. 2.9; Trinity Sunday: John 1.14 and Rev. 7.12; Saints' Days: Eph. 1.14 and Heb. 12.2 and 1 Pet. 5.4; Dedication: 1 Kings 8.29, Eph. 2.20–2, and 2 Cor. 5.1.

Breaking of the Bread (Section 30)
1 Cor. 10.16–17.

Benedictus and Agnus Dei (Section 34)
Matt. 21.9; John 1.29 and 1 Pet. 1.18–20.

Sentences after Communion (Section 37)
Advent: Rev. 22.20; Christmas: John 6.33; Lent: Luke 22.28, 30; Passiontide: 1 Cor. 11.26; Easter: John 6.54; Ascension: Phil. 2.9–10; Whitsun: Rom. 8.11; Trinity Sunday: 1 Pet. 1.2; Saints' Days: Heb. 12.22–4; Dedication: 1 Kings 8.27; Unity: Eph. 2.18.

Prayer after Communion (Section 39)
Luke 15.5, 20; Isa. 26.2; Ps. 118.19; 1 Cor. 12.27; Col. 3.1; Mark 10.38–9; Matt. 5.14–16; Luke 11.36; Acts 13.47; Heb. 6.19–20; Isa. 45.22; Ps. 66.4.

Seasonal Blessings (Section 42)
Advent: Mal. 4.2 and 1 John 1.5; Christmas: Mark 1.14–15; Lent: Wisd. 1.5 and Matt. 16.24; Passiontide: John 12.32 and Heb. 6.19, 11; 10.22; Easter: Heb. 13.20; Ascension: Rom. 2.7 and 2 Tim. 2.12; Whitsun: John 16.13 and Phil. 2.11 and 2 Tim. 4.2; Trinity Sunday: Rom. 4.20, Ps. 20.1, Judg. 8.34, and John 16.13; Saints' Days: 1 Cor. 13.13; Unity: John 10.11, 16.

First published in 1971
Second impression 1971
Third impression 1971
Fourth impression 1971
S.P.C.K., Holy Trinity Church, Marylebone Road, London NW1 4DU

Printed in Great Britain by The Talbot Press (S.P.C.K.), Saffron Walden, Essex

© The Registrars of the Provinces of Canterbury and York, 1971

SBN 281 02660 2